To shun simulacra and representations, to wrest oneself out of the theater one has made of one's life, out of the roles: the lover or the father, the boss, the king, the conqueror, the pauper, the little girl or the prostitute, the soothsayer and the great actress, everything, everything that has made us dream so much ever since our childhood, to cast it all off, to drop our imaginary clothes and run naked.

Antoine Vitez

an Archeology of Fear and Desire

Frédéric Brenner

Jerusalem   2010

Hebron Road   2011

Judean Hills   2009

Rachel's Tomb   2010

Sodom   2010

Ben Gurion Airport   2010

Border Police Unit   2010

Shlomi and Oren   2012

Hadera   2013

Al Baladiya   2010

Muhammad   2010

Rinat   2010

Kanimer Makoria   2010

Talia Rosin   2010

Identity Undisclosed   2011

Netiv HaAsara   2010

Elior Brenner   2009

Ruth Chaya Leonov-Carmely, Nechama Weitman, Pnina Leonov   2010

Kibbutz Ma'agan Michael   2012

The Dead Sea   2010

Hany and Ya'akov Ben-David   2009

The Aslan Levi Family   2010

Sderot   2011

Menashe Testimony Theater   2013

Rothschild Boulevard   2012

Liberty Bell Garden   2010

Snir Stream Laguna   2010

The Weinfeld Family   2009

The Awad Family   2011

The Hatuel Family   2012

Mitzpe Modi'in   2011

Tel Aviv   2011

An Archeology of Fear and Desire is an attempt to fathom the cauldron of fear and shadow within each of us, unrecognised, unredeemed, denied, dissimulated and silenced, where the other is instrumentalised and thereby sacrificed. It is an essay about devouring myths and how constructs, social and religious, perpetuate a tyranny of roles which render us strangers to what is most intimate in us. It is about the fiction of identity, about longing, belonging, exclusion and redemption. It is an attempt to recontextualise Israel as place and metaphor and to look anew at a territory where, in the words of philosopher Moshe Halbertal, 'the maps of the sacred overlap, compete and ultimately exclude each other.' Wrestling and embracing…

In 2005, alone at home in Paris, I imagined inviting artists from around the world to come to Israel and use their cameras, neither to praise nor condemn, but to question and reveal. That improbable adventure became a reality thanks to the generosity and vision of hundreds of people who embraced the project as their own, contributing time, money, a room to stay or film to shoot and most importantly, their ideas and daring spirit. This project brought me a true embarrassment of riches, too many friends and supporters to name in this short space, but please know that I am endlessly grateful to you.

An Archeology of Fear and Desire is my own photographic contribution to *This Place*, and I would especially like to thank those who have been instrumental in the creation and selection of these images. To my assistants, Lior Avitan and Oren Myers, who brought insight, technical expertise and wide-ranging talents, thank you for sharing the joys and frustrations of making images. I also want to thank the photographers, curators, and other arts professionals who took the time to look at these images with a combination of generosity and rigor that is a gift to any artist: Wendy Ewald, Martin Kollar, Josef Koudelka, Jungjin Lee, Gilles Peress, Fazal Sheikh, Rosalind Solomon, Stephen Shore, Thomas Struth, Jeff Wall, Nick Waplington, Charlotte Cotton, Howard Greenberg, Michael Mack, Grégoire Pujade-Lauraine, Jeff Rosenheim, and Urs Stahel. I am also deeply indebted to the people I photographed. You were my inspiration; my photographs emerged from our encounters, and we created them in partnership.

To Matthew Brogan and Bonnie Boxer, you were my closest and most trusted collaborators. Without you, there simply would have been no project. Nor would I have succeeded without Hamutal Waisel's ethical intelligence and logistic magic.

To my sister Carine Brenner and my mother Denise Brenner, you shared your bountiful tables and wonderful cooking with all my guests. Your generosity added so much humanity to the project and you, Carine, were instrumental in testing and refining my ideas.

Finally and especially, to Hetty Berg, my partner and my enabler.

An Archeology of Fear and Desire is part of a project entitled *This Place*, which explores the complexity of Israel and the West Bank through the eyes of twelve internationally acclaimed photographers, their highly individual works combining to create not a single, monolithic vision, but rather a diverse and fragmented portrait, alive to the rifts and paradoxes of this important and much contested place. *This Place* consists of a travelling exhibition, companion publications and a program of live events.

this-place.org

Frontispiece: Palace Hotel, 2009

First edition published by MACK

© 2014 MACK for this edition
© 2014 Frédéric Brenner for the images
Antoine Vitez extract from 'I was a child, I was reading Peer Gynt'

MACK
mackbooks.co.uk

ISBN 9781910164006